6/03

John —

Happy 50 !

Hope you e

little book

your friendship is priceless.

Live Well —

David

PRESENTED TO:

BY:

The LITTLE BOOK OF BIG QUESTIONS

by
Dianna Booher

Illustrated by Michelle Allen

COUNTRYMAN®

FOREWORD

Have you ever had a child whose dog died look you in the eye and ask, "Is Buddy in heaven now?" Or have you ever tried to comfort a friend stricken with cancer who questions why she has to endure such pain and suffering?

And what about the questions that society continually poses: What ever happened to personal responsibility? Does our judicial system still work? Does God really help those who help themselves— or does He help those who can't help themselves?

Finally, there are your own questions. What is the true measure of success? Is there really life after death? What makes a good marriage? How do I know when I have enough money to retire?

I hope this book creates food for thought as you grapple with both the simple and the significant issues in life. In the right place, at the right time, in the right relationship, you may find these thoughts helpful in affecting someone's outlook, attitude—or eternal destiny.

Dianna Booher
March, 1999

You don't need to know all the answers. No one is smart enough yet to ask you all the questions.

— ANONYMOUS

WHAT MAKES PEOPLE WISH FOR THINGS THEY DON'T HAVE?

Contentment works like hunger. People often experience emptiness despite what they have. They have a huge hole in their heart for something that's satisfying, and they're trying to fill it with the wrong things. If you can't be content with what you have, at least be thankful for what you have escaped.

It's not how much we have, but how much we enjoy what we have, that makes for happiness. —CHARLES SPURGEON

WHY ARE OTHERWISE RESERVED PEOPLE WILLING TO TELL STRANGERS ON AN AIRPLANE INTIMATE DETAILS ABOUT THEIR LIVES?

If you are not a charming conversationalist, you may still be a big hit as a charmed listener.

— ANONYMOUS

They assume anonymity and objectivity. But given our global workplace and our Internet connections, travelers would do well to rethink this conclusion. Short of aliases and assumed identities, chances favor our crossing paths again. As for objectivity, I've never met an unbiased individual with no frame of reference.

In our country, the Constitution guarantees free speech; it doesn't guarantee listeners. Most of us grab them where we can.

What's the Best Age in Life?

Age is irrelevant. Opportunity, health, relationships, and state of mind are the best predictors of genuine contentment.

Age is not important unless you're a cheese.

— HELEN HAYES

WHAT IS THE BEST MEASURE OF THE GREATNESS OF A SOCIETY?

- The way they treat their youngest and oldest citizens.

- The opportunity they offer to outsiders.

- The leaders they choose to follow.

- How they honor their dead.

The fate of America cannot depend on any one man. The greatness of America is grounded in principles and not on any single personality.
— FRANKLIN D. ROOSEVELT

When were the good and the brave ever in a majority?
— HENRY DAVID THOREAU

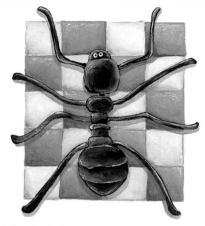

DOES GOD REALLY HELP THOSE WHO HELP THEMSELVES, OR HELP THOSE WHO CAN'T HELP THEMSELVES?

Both. God provides talent, opportunity, and energy for people to help themselves. For those who can't help themselves, He teaches them dependence. Their weakness showcases His strength.

Go to the ant, you sluggard! Consider her ways and be wise, which, having no captain, overseer or ruler, provides her supplies in the summer and gathers her food in the harvest.
— PROVERBS 6:6-7

WHY DOES MONEY MAKE SOME PEOPLE PROUD AND OTHERS HUMBLE?

Some wealthy people think their riches came to them by their own cunning, wisdom, expertise, and effort. They mistake the power and persuasion of money for true popularity and purpose. They compare their fortune and status in life with those who know less, do less, and have less.

Wiser wealthy people look at their riches through the eyes of gratitude. They realize that they were born with their intellect intact. They understand that family, teachers, spouses, or associates have fostered a climate that encourages making the best use of what they've been given. They realize their dependence on God for good health. They compare their fortune and status in life with those who've known more, done more, and worked harder—with fewer financial rewards.

IS THERE SUCH A THING AS THE GENERATION GAP?

It's growing wider every day: Young people think that intelligence, energy, and determination are a substitute for experience. Older people think that experience is a substitute for intelligence, energy, and determination.

Two things can bridge the gap: love and laughter. Too many of the young haven't learned to love. Too many of the old have forgotten how to laugh.

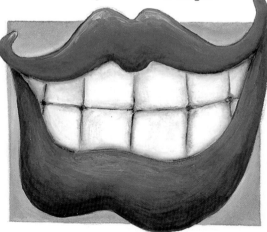

Paradoxical as it may seem, to believe in youth is to look backward; to look forward we must believe in age.
— DOROTHY L. SAYERS

WHY DO THINGS ALWAYS LOOK BETTER IN THE MORNING?

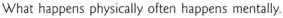

Have you ever slept outside? You feel the air cool against your skin. The morning sun thrusts its radiant yellow rays toward the blue sky. You stretch your limbs and feel shot through with a thousand watts of energy.

What happens physically often happens mentally.

For one thing, life's rituals train us to wake up to action in the morning. As children, we get up and dress to go to school. As adults, we get dressed to go to work or to face the day at home. Action follows the night's inertia.

For another thing, the morning sunlight serves as an analogy for a new beginning. Whatever happened yesterday is gone; the sunlight spells a new day for new undertakings, new insights, new resolutions.

For another thing, we're rested. Much like a car that spits and sputters on a cold morning, when we shake off the physical sluggishness, our mental motor starts to purr.

It's morning. There's sunlight. There's movement. There's time.

IS THERE REALLY SOMEONE FOR EVERYONE?

As long as there is hope in the human heart, people dream of romance. There IS someone for everyone. The difficulty is finding the RIGHT someone. And the difficulty in finding the RIGHT someone depends on the length of your shopping list and the places you shop.

Love is blind; friendship closes its eyes.
— FRENCH PROVERB

Most of us want very much to be loved. Perhaps we are not concerned enough about loving.
— ERWIN MCDONALD

WHAT'S THE DIFFERENCE BETWEEN LEGAL AND RIGHT?

Right is right, no matter who's against it. Wrong is wrong, no matter who's for it. Legal simply means that more people and politicians are for it than against it.

Of all the lessons history teaches, this one is plainest: the person who tries to achieve ends through force is always unscrupulous and is always cruel. We should remember this in an age where morality seems to be disappearing and is being replaced by politics.
—EUSTACE PERCY

IS IT GOOD FOR PEOPLE TO BE DEEPLY ATTACHED TO PETS?

Certainly. We could learn a thing or two from our pets. Consider these habits:

- Be quiet around those who've had a hard day
- Sit close, nuzzle, whimper when they do, and stare sympathetically
- Refresh yourself by going out for a walk and fresh air
- Run and play daily
- Take a nap when you're tired
- Stretch before jumping into full action
- Rush to greet those you love
- Dig until you find your own bone
- Protect your personal space and let others know when they violate it
- Be loyal to those you love

We don't say what we mean often because we don't know what we think and feel. Our thinking and feeling are fuzzy. If we say what we think, we may hurt someone's feelings. If we think we may hurt someone's feelings, we obscure the message. If we obscure the message, others miss the point. If others miss the point, they ignore it. If they ignore it, nothing changes. If nothing changes, they're off the hook. If they're off the hook, we're blameless. If we're blameless, we can at least say we "tried."

WHY DON'T WE SAY WHAT WE MEAN?

The greatest problem with communication is the illusion that it has been accomplished.
    — GEORGE BERNARD SHAW

Some people use language to express thought, some to conceal thought, and others instead of thought.
    — ANONYMOUS

HOW DO COLORS AND MUSIC CHANGE OUR MOODS?

Colors and music seep into our subconscious to soothe or seduce our soul. Red or blaring trumpets can trigger our anger or angst. Blue or violins can calm our nerves. Green or drums can invigorate us with energy and determined action.

It's both amusing and amazing that music and colors may have more power over us than great ideas or wise friends.

WHY IS THE BIBLE STILL THE BEST-SELLING BOOK OF ALL TIME?

To the sick and dying, it offers comfort.

To the depressed, it provides hope.

To the joyful, it explains their exuberance.

To the fearful, its panorama of history builds confidence for the future.

To the restless, it gives a sense of purpose.

For friend or family, it offers therapy for damaged relationships.

For the employee or employer, it provides instruction for daily decisions.

For the prisoner, it pricks the conscience and shows a better path.

To the poor, it promises intangible riches.

To the rich, it encourages grace, gratitude, and giving.

To the unimportant, it gives significance.

To the famous, it suggests humility.

To the intellectual, it feeds the mind with profound truths.

IS THERE LIFE ON OTHER PLANETS?

The Bible does not specifically address the issue of our human term *planets*. Rather, it speaks of all of creation being brought into existence through God's work, by His plan, and for His purpose. Whether we discover other planets and other civilizations will be determined by whether God allows us that access.

The bigger question now seems to be, *What are we doing with the civilization we have?* Why concern ourselves with life on another planet . . . until we improve the life of all within our sphere of influence on earth?

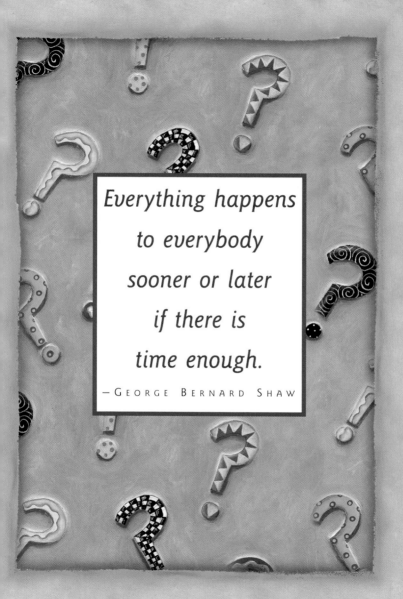

Everything happens to everybody sooner or later if there is time enough.

—GEORGE BERNARD SHAW

WHY DO WE EAT AFTER FUNERALS?

If death represents
freedom from the
hardships or sickness
of this life, it is a
celebration to be
freed to the hereafter.
Food is the focal
point of most
celebrations.

WHICH IS MORE DEPENDABLE IN DECISION-MAKING— INSTINCT OR LOGIC?

The man who insists upon seeing with perfect clearness before he decides, never decides.
— HENRI-FREDERIC AMIEL

Instinct or logic? That depends on your purpose, awareness, and habits. Your logic and your instincts work on two different levels, one conscious and one subconscious. If you're typically aware of the source of your emotions and mentally give yourself permission to use your "gut" for decisions, your instincts can gather and analyze information quickly. Your emotions react to body language, subtle clues in things said or not said, in a physical reaction to environment, circumstances, and people.

On the other hand, those who are unaware of their own emotional perceptions typically gather information in a more conscious way, using the mind's reasoning apparatus. They tend to exclude information coming to them from the emotional, subconscious source.

Both instinct and logic (the conscious and subconscious) can be equally valuable sources of information and guidance for decision-making.

WHY DOES POWER IMPROVE SOME PEOPLE AND CORRUPT OTHERS?

When people are full of ego, pride, resentment, revenge, greed, or ambition, little can restrain them from using the power they gain for their own ends.

But power does not necessarily produce pleasure. Nor is power alone proof of wisdom or greatness.

The highest test of character is to have limitless power without abusing it. Power can break other people's spirits or win their hearts. The powerfully wise have chosen the nobler purpose.

The love of liberty is the love of others; the love of power is the love of ourselves.
— WILLIAM HAZLITT

The lust for power is not rooted in strength but in weakness.
— ERICH FROMM

DOES PRAYER REALLY WORK?

Ask those who've been healed of cancer.

Ask soldiers who've fought a war and returned to tell about it.

Ask those intellectuals who've studied philosophies around the world and found peace only in personal faith.

Ask those who've raised great kids while living in Harlem.

Ask those who now love a spouse when once there was hatred and distrust.

Ask those whose businesses have made a dramatic turnaround, from bankruptcy to success.

Ask those who've been penniless and now live in luxury.

Ask those who've been guilty and now feel forgiven.

Ask those who've been bitter and now feel love.

The effective, fervent prayer of a righteous man avails much.
— J A M E S 5 : 1 6

WHAT'S THE FINE LINE BETWEEN SEEING THAT YOUR NEEDS ARE MET AND BEING SELFISH?

If you are living for yourself, you work and play in a small universe. And like other small pursuits and pleasures, self-centeredness gets boring rather quickly. Worse, you will be a slave to the greatest slave if you serve only yourself.

Need is another issue altogether. Even Jesus withdrew from the needy crowds on occasion. You must meet your emotional, physical, or spiritual needs, otherwise you have no resources to give out to others— no skills, no expertise, no information, no ideas, no energy, no wisdom, no love.

Intention and timing are everything. If you get to give, you become a channel, not a dam.

The person who is all wrapped up in himself is overdressed.
— ANONYMOUS

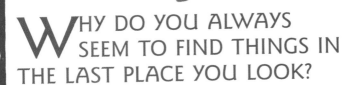

WHY DO YOU ALWAYS SEEM TO FIND THINGS IN THE LAST PLACE YOU LOOK?

When you find them, you stop looking.

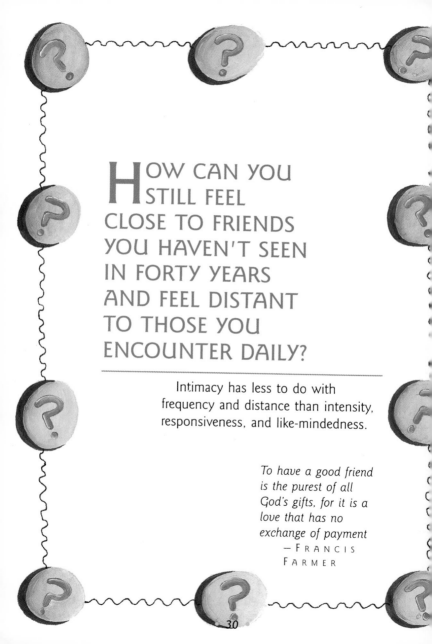

How can you still feel close to friends you haven't seen in forty years and feel distant to those you encounter daily?

Intimacy has less to do with frequency and distance than intensity, responsiveness, and like-mindedness.

To have a good friend is the purest of all God's gifts, for it is a love that has no exchange of payment
— FRANCIS FARMER

WHAT IS A GOOD MARRIAGE?

Married couples know they've met their soul mate in marriage if . . .

one is absolutely right on an issue and then lets the matter drop.

they still laugh at each other's jokes.

they'd rather spend Saturday afternoons together than apart.

they show each other the common courtesies offered to complete strangers.

they can argue until they're blue in the face and still eat pizza together before bedtime.

they feel free to point out each other's faults and help each other improve.

they can sense when something's bothering the other without a spoken word.

they can talk about any topic without the other leaving the room.

one is always willing to give up something for the other—and the other won't allow it.

they not only look forward to staying young together but look forward to growing old together.

Sure, time means progress, but . . .

- We've conquered smallpox, tuberculosis, and lock-jaw—but what about AIDS, multiple sclerosis, and the common cold?

DOES TIME MEAN PROGRESS?

- We've torn down the Iron Curtain and split the Soviet Union—but what about the Serbs, the Somalians, and the Sudanese?

- We've connected the globe with the Internet—but do we contact our senators about issues that will affect our future?

- We've taught our kids about safe sex—but have we taught them when and why?

- We've passed child-labor laws to take kids out of the factories—but when are we going to get them off the streets?

- We've taught people to harness technology—but can technology prevent an earthquake?

- We've taught people how to make more money—but have we taught them to give to those who have less?

- We've taught people how to make a living—but have we taught them what makes life significant?

HOW CAN YOU STOP WORRYING?

One negative outcome to an education is that it enables us to worry more intelligently about global issues and the unpredictable future. That being the case, worry never robs tomorrow of its problems—it only saps today of its strength.

Trade worry time for

problem analysis . . .

preparation . . .

prayer . . .

and praise.

Do not worry about your life, what you will eat or what you will drink; nor about your body, what you will put on. Is not life more than food, and the body more than clothing? Look at the birds of the air, for they neither sow nor reap nor gather into barns; yet your heavenly Father feeds them. Are you not of more value than they? Which of you by worrying can add one cubit to his stature?

— MATTHEW 6 : 2 5 - 2 7 .

Credibility stems from that elusive thing called perception. People's perception of you may be based on what they hear others say about you, the way you talk and act, or their previous experiences with people like you. Credibility is based on a track record—either real or perceived.

WHY DO SOME PEOPLE HAVE MORE CREDIBILITY AND INFLUENCE THAN OTHERS?

Those who are most credible over the long haul—

- tell the truth

- do what they say they will

- behave consistently—their actions match their words

- show concern and compassion for others

- demonstrate knowledge and skill

- exercise good judgment and make good decisions for all concerned

- stand strong on their values

- motivate others to be and do the best they can

HOW DO YOU DISTINGUISH BETWEEN GUIDANCE THAT COMES FROM YOUR OWN INTENTIONS AND GUIDANCE THAT'S DIVINELY INSPIRED?

If you pour water into a clean bucket, it's likely the water will remain pure. But pour water into a contaminated bucket and the water becomes part of the residue. In the same way, we are like contaminated receptacles, full of our own thoughts, intentions, motives, likes, and dislikes. Ideas, motives, and decisions that pop from our  own minds come from either reasoning or rationalization. They rarely contradict our personal emotions or wills. It's difficult not to mix our thoughts with divine inspiration.

So how can you distinguish between the two? (1) The Word of God; (2) the circumstances you find yourself in; (3) and peace of mind about your course of action—when all three of these are consistent, you will find yourself operating on inspiration, not exasperation.

WHAT IS THE TRUE MEASURE OF SUCCESS?

Your best. Nothing less. In all things, success should be determined by contribution, not accumulation.

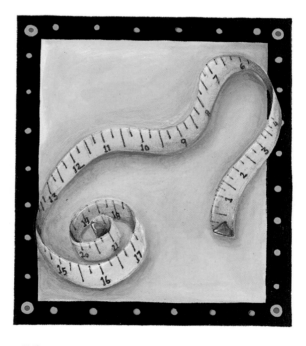

Whatever you can do, or dream you can, begin it.
— J. W. VON GOETHE

DOES GOD REALLY HEAL PEOPLE?

God heals those He chooses to heal. His ways are not our ways, and our ways are not His ways. At times, He's worked His healing through doctors and medicine. At other times, He's healed people through miraculous reversals of scientific principles and natural laws. He heals based on the prayers and faith of those who are sick—and sometimes based on the faith of those families and friends praying on behalf of the unbelieving sick.

He has also healed the unbelieving in His merciful attempt to give people one more chance to respond to His love and commit their future life to His kingdom's work and purpose. His love and compassion are often incomprehensible.

WHAT'S THE DIFFERENCE BETWEEN A STRONG WORK ETHIC AND WORKAHOLISM?

Attitude and purpose. The work ethic generally flows from our inclination to give away. Workaholism, on the other hand, comes from what we're trying to avoid. Motive and balance separate the two.

We've come from the Puritan work ethic to the new work ethic, from living to work to working to live. The current work attitude among younger people: you have a job you want done. I have a life I want to live. Let's make a deal.

— ROGER
   BLACKWELL

I've been working all my life, but somehow it seems longer.
— ROBERT
   ORBEN

CAN YOU BE A SPIRITUAL PERSON AND WORSHIP GOD WITHOUT EVER GOING TO CHURCH, TEMPLE, OR SYNAGOGUE?

It's possible, but not probable. It's possible to be aware of your spiritual nature, reflect on spiritual truths, and respond to spiritual promptings in any place at any time for any reason. But consider the realities.

When people go to an amusement park on vacation, they're in the mood to play. People who check into the hospital for surgery have made a commitment to undergo whatever is necessary to get well. Guests at a party expect to network and have fun. For all the same reasons, people who attend a place of worship find encouragement and an atmosphere that's conducive to worship.

Worship anywhere, anytime, with anyone is possible. But the reality is rare.

We are *most likely* to recognize our spiritual needs, reflect on our shortcomings and our potentials, and respond to these urgings for change when surrounded by people of like purpose, people who encourage us for reasons that we value.

WHY DO PEOPLE DO THE "BAD STUFF" THAT IS HARMFUL TO THEMSELVES RATHER THAN THE "GOOD STUFF" THAT IS HELPFUL?

The short list on "bad stuff" comes down to drugs, dangerous stunts, depressing and defeatist thinking. The short list on "good stuff" includes nutritional eating, ample rest, appropriate exercise, stimulating reading, and imaginative thinking.

We succumb to the bad stuff when we do not exercise self-discipline. We drift rather than determine. We dawdle rather than decide. We dream rather than deliver.

When we fail to control ourselves, the danger is that someone else will. And the greatest danger of all? That *no one* else will.

You can't turn back
the clock, but you
can wind it up again.

—Bonnie Prudden

IS IT OKAY TO TELL "SMALL" LIES TO HELP OTHERS SAVE FACE OR FEEL BETTER?

Facts and information should stand alone, as naked truth to be shared openly and in kindness with noble intentions. Opinions, stated positively as such and without malice, tend to focus others in a new direction. They offer hope while confirming value in the other person.

The greatest damage results, however, when we state our *negative* opinions as if they were *unalterable facts.*

When the only choice left is a lie, prefer silence.

If you have generations of leaders lying to people, the truth becomes debased, and a lot of values fall by the wayside as well.
— HILLARY RODHAM CLINTON

WHY DOESN'T GOD KEEP BAD THINGS FROM HAPPENING TO GOOD PEOPLE?

For those who like to reason, consider these . . .

- God doesn't originate bad things.

- To randomly reverse natural laws would create more bad things. For example, the same drought that causes cotton and wheat to die causes grapes to grow. Nature is God's creation, not His toy.

- Bad things come from free will in the world; to limit bad things would restrict personal freedom.

- Not all suffering is bad. While suffering tests our faith, it can also build our character. The philosophy that all of life should be pleasurable is called hedonism.

- People who endure bad things well teach others lessons about grace, strength, and commitment.

- Some "bad things" turn out not to be not so bad after all.

- God sometimes allows bad things to achieve a greater good.

The real problem is not why some pious, humble, believing people suffer, but why some do not.
— C . S . L E W I S

WHAT IS THE PURPOSE OF LIFE?

From the fluttering butterfly to the flowing lava, consider the creativity in creation. Humans are a little lower than the angels, higher than animals and fauna, with inquiring minds to question their own existence. That questioning itself is the strongest evidence of a soul.

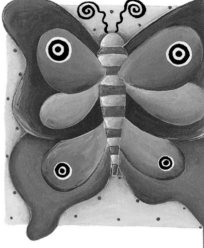

The purpose of life is to enjoy fellowship with God now and in the hereafter. While we're doing so, He allows us to serve as His hands on earth. That purpose and mission allows us to live a meaningful existence full of peace, purpose, and hope.

Nothing contributes so much to tranquilize the mind as a steady purpose—a point on which the soul may fix its intellectual eye.
— MARY SHELLY WOLLSTONECRAFT

IS THERE LIFE AFTER DEATH?

Testing the various philosophies about God and eternity, I used to play "what if" games. I'd pose this question to a friend: "What if you're right and I'm wrong? What if I live all my life believing there's a God and an eternity and in the end discover that I'm wrong? What happens to me then?"

The answer came back: "No problem. We're both mounds of dust forever."

"Okay," I'd respond. "Not so bad. I end up just like everybody else, a nothing."

Then I'd pose the second question to my friend: "What if I'm right and you're wrong? What if you live all your life believing there is no God and no eternity and in the end discover that you're wrong? What then?"

Isn't the fact that we cannot imagine our own nonexistence evidence itself of eternity? Why wait to step over into eternity? We're already in it.

All that's not eternal is out of date.
— C. S. Lewis

HOW CAN YOU FEEL LOVE FOR SOMEONE YOU SOMETIMES DON'T EVEN LIKE?

Romantic love is based on physical attraction.

Brotherly love tickles our personalities and our mutual motives.

Agape love wells up inside us even when our personalities clash or our passion fades. Agape love comes from a source outside ourselves for a purpose larger than ourselves. It is over-the-shoulder love for under-the-counter support.

When love opens the hearts of others, words and understanding seep in.

God's love elevates us without inflating us, and humbles us without degrading us.

— B. M. NOTTAGE

WHY DO SOME PEOPLE REFUSE TO LEARN FROM OTHER PEOPLE'S EXPERIENCES?

They always think they will be different somehow. They think . . .

- the details of their situation will change the outcome.

- they'll have more control over a situation.

- they'll not feel the same pressure and stress.

- they'll have more knowledge or information.

- their timing will be more appropriate.

- their luck will run better.

- they'll be more careful.

- others are more stupid.

Experience will be the cheapest yet most valuable thing you can use in life—if you decide to get it second-hand.

SECOND HAND

WHAT'S THE DIFFERENCE BETWEEN NUDITY AND PORNOGRAPHY?

Intent, purpose, and result.

Nudity is

a naked victim of an earthquake.

a wounded solider lying in the street.

a newborn baby at bath time.

a couple making love.

Pornography is

nudity meant to arouse illicit sexual passion.

nudity displayed for the sake of making money.

nudity that results in leading someone to do something immoral.

The argument that pornography cannot be censored without destroying our civil liberties is fundamentally wrong. We have censored pornography since the nation was established, and there is no evidence of an adverse effect on our civil liberties.
— WINTON M. BLOUNT

WHERE DID HUMANS COME FROM?

The mind, heart, and hands of God.

In the beginning was the Word, and the Word was with God, and the Word was God. He was in the beginning with God. All things were made through Him, and without Him nothing was made that was made.

—JOHN 1:1

WHY DO THE PUNCTUAL PEOPLE IN THE WORLD MARRY THE LAID-BACK PEOPLE?

The guy who'd rather be half an hour early to a meeting than two minutes late generally marries a woman who doesn't start her make-up until time to leave the house. I know a woman who can write a legal brief in the time it takes her husband to write a check. You see these couples everywhere.

What is the attraction? The laid-back types yearn for the discipline and organization of the punctual. The punctual types long for the spontaneity of those who "let things happen." Neither the laid-back types nor the punctual types will give up their own habits and attitudes long enough to grasp hold of the opposite way of thinking, but as long as they marry an opposite, they have a fifty-fifty chance of having it both ways.

HOW DO YOU KNOW WHEN YOU'RE INTERFERING IN SOMEONE'S LIFE?

How often do you get invited back? Consider that the person who often asks your advice may be looking for affirmation and confirmation rather than information.

The two quickest ways to disaster are to take nobody's advice and to take everybody's advice.
— DUBLIN OPINION

It takes a great man to give sound advice tactfully, but a greater to accept it graciously.
— J. C. MACULAY

WHY DO WE TREAT THOSE WE LOVE WORSE THAN WE TREAT COMPLETE STRANGERS?

We assume those we love will forgive us. Given the same bad treatment, complete strangers would hold us accountable, reject us, or punish us. As a consequence, we give complete strangers clout and control in matters that are off limits to our loved ones.

Should we continue to treat those we love worse than complete strangers, eventually, they will *become* complete strangers.

DO MIRACLES STILL HAPPEN?

Ask the parents of a newborn.

Ask the person who has cancer in remission.

Ask the father whose rebellious teenager has returned home with respect and a positive attitude.

Ask an entrepreneur who started with scratch and now runs a $200 billion company.

Ask the person who once felt despair but now feels hope.

Anyone who doesn't believe in miracles is not a realist.
— DAVID BEN-GURION

HOW HAS OUR THROW-AWAY SOCIETY AFFECTED PERSONAL RESPONSIBILITY?

As consumers, we've learned that it's faster, cheaper, easier to discard and replace than to repair and reuse. We've replaced the genuine and permanent for the temporary and disposable—in diapers, dishes, and dogma. We've expanded the objects-are-worthless philosophy to include life. The conclusion then follows that if life itself has little or no value, our individual behavior is of no consequence.

While three-fifths of the world's population worries about hunger and survival, we anxiously wrestle with overweight and boredom. Every newspaper supplies increasing evidence that in terms of gross national product, comfort, and personal income, we are . . . superior. . . . Yet, in personal relationships and inner peace, we are revealing that we do not know how to live. We are artists at having and failures at being.
— CHARLES GARRIGUS

WHY IS ENGLISH SO ILLOGICAL?

Our language is a hodge-podge of prefixes, suffixes, and roots from several languages. As a result, we have endless combinations with contradictory meanings. We drive on parkways and park on driveways. Our apartments are stuck together. Our houses stand apart. Our airplanes have "near misses" when they have not collided at all.

The plural of tooth is teeth, but the plural of booth is not beeth. The plural of mouse is mice, but the plural of noose is not nice. A slim chance and a fat chance mean the same. So do inflammable and flammable. But a wise man and wise guy are contradictory. Button and unbutton are opposites, but ravel and unravel mean the same.

We spell the same "f" sound four ways: *fun*, *gruff*, *phone*, *enough*. Then we take the same word spelled the same way and pronounce it to mean different things: recover and re-cover.

If a skater skates, a singer sings, a painter paints, and a teacher teachers, why doesn't a violinist *violin*?

It's a wonder we communicate at all!

WHY DO SOME PEOPLE ENJOY A LIFE OF EASE WHILE OTHERS SUFFER POVERTY AND ABUSE?

A life of ease does not signify a life of meaning. Neither does a life of poverty, abuse, or suffering rule out joy or reward. A life of ease may be a sign of God's blessings—or evidence of our uselessness. A life of tragedy may be the consequence of other's poor choices—or a showcase for God's grace and provision despite those choices.

The easy and the difficult provide contrast from which our appreciation and understanding grow. How can we understand happiness if we've never known sadness? How can we appreciate plenty if we've never known need? How can we recognize rest if we've never known weariness?

Our reaction to the ease or the difficulty makes the strongest statement to the world.

Do not pray for easy lives. Pray to be stronger men. Do not pray for tasks equal to your powers. Pray for powers equal to your tasks.
— PHILLIPS BROOKS

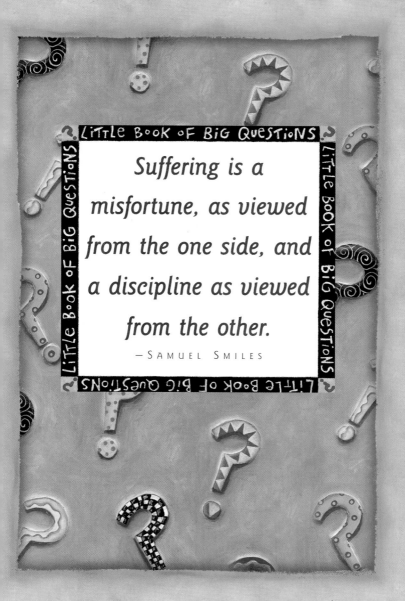

LiTTLE BooK oF BiG QuESTioNS

Suffering is a misfortune, as viewed from the one side, and a discipline as viewed from the other.

—SAMUEL SMILES

WHERE HAVE ALL THE ROLE MODELS GONE?

Sports figures and entertainers garner more admiration from young people worldwide than any other professionals. Yet many have made their primary message Brand X shoes or Brand Y coffee. What if all these role models spent their spare time persuading kids to avoid drugs, study hard in school, and respect those in authority?

Many professionals in all walks of life have become so focused on themselves that they refuse to accept the responsibility that comes with success—responsibility to walk circumspectly before the younger generation, which needs someone marking the way and leaving a trail.

We can't all be heroes, because someone has to sit on the curb and clap as they go by.
  — WILL ROGERS

DOES OUR JUDICIAL SYSTEM STILL WORK?

All virtue is summed up in dealing justly.
— ARISTOTLE

Laws too gentle are seldom obeyed; too severe, seldom executed.
— BENJAMIN FRANKLIN

Common sense often makes good law.
— WILLIAM O. DOUGLAS

A mandatory life-sentence automatically commutes to forty years. Someone who kills a cat receives twelve years in prison, while a couple who kills a child gets two years. Why? Those jurists who hold influential jobs, who are informed about cases of national interest, and who analyze and hold opinions about social issues are struck from the jury box. Our judges serve based on their political affiliations and preferences and at the mercy of public opinion. Verdicts often turn on the fame and fortune of the accused. Wrong wins by technicalities.

Our legal system may be the best in the world, but truth considered, we should drop the label "justice" from the process.

Golf is a game of ambiance: etiquette, emotion, equality. It compasses small courtesies despite the competition. Players experience the roller-coaster highs on a long drive that lands inches from the hole; they need encouragement for the sand traps. A ten-year-old can play against a sixty-year-old on equal footing. It involves attention to detail on every shot while demanding consistency for the entire course. And the scoreboard often depends on character.

WHAT IS THE WORLD'S FASCINATION WITH GOLF?

The most difficult part of golf is learning not to talk about it.
— ANONYMOUS

IS IT RIGHT TO LET PEOPLE IN OTHER COUNTRIES STARVE?

Is a gift not a gift if it's not accepted? Starvation stems from decisions, drought, or dementia. Rulers and warring factions become the filters for food the world offers. How hard should outsiders push to get through these filters? The answer lies in our willingness to sacrifice our own citizens when we meet an unwelcome shoreline.

I have come to believe that the one thing people cannot bear is a sense of injustice. Poverty, cold, even hunger, are more bearable than injustice.

— MILLICENT FENWICK

DOES TIME HEAL ALL WOUNDS?

No. Some wounds only fester. Some have to be punctured and drained before they scab over.

Sorrow, like rain, makes roses and mud.
— AUSTIN O'MALLEY

Believe me, every heart has its secret sorrows, which the world knows not; and oftentimes we call a man cold when he is only sad.
— HENRY W. LONGFELLOW

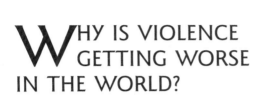

WHY IS VIOLENCE GETTING WORSE IN THE WORLD?

Violence is the expression of anger turned outward with force. It is an eruption of frustration for real or imagined wrongs done by parents, teachers, bosses, or other authority figures.

As our culture shuns personal responsibility for actions and decisions,
　　as our leaders refuse to be role models,
　　　　as we value technology more than humans,
　　　　　as materialism replaces spirituality,
　　　　　　as our future grows bleaker,
　　　　　　　. . . our value for the
　　　　　　　　　　individual declines.

Violence is the result of anonymity, mixed with rage, void of thought, adrift without purpose.

What is hurting America today is the high cost of low living.
— BROOKS MOORE

WHAT ARE THE PLEASURES AND DEMANDS OF FREEDOM?

Freedom is a package deal—with it come responsibilities and consequences. Freedom includes rights, riches, and reasoning. Responsibilities demand time, effort, and noble intentions. Consequences cost money, mistakes, and misfortunes.

The freedom of any group of people can best be measured by the volume of its laughter. How often, how loud, and how long do you laugh?

Freedom is not the right to do as you please, but the liberty to do as you ought.
—EUGENE P. BERTIN

WHY DOES SOCIETY PAY ENTERTAINERS AND SPORTS FIGURES MORE THAN TEACHERS?

We don't put our money where our mouth is. When asked about their values, most people would give accolades to teachers who mold the thinking and attitudes of the younger generation while preparing them with skills and knowledge for a life of success.

Yet when deciding where to spend their discretionary income, most people would prefer to buy a ticket to the ballgame than write a check to their local school.

In contests of priorities and pocketbooks, economics and pleasure triumph over values.

It is not what is poured into the student, but what is planted, that counts.
— EUGENE P. BERTIN

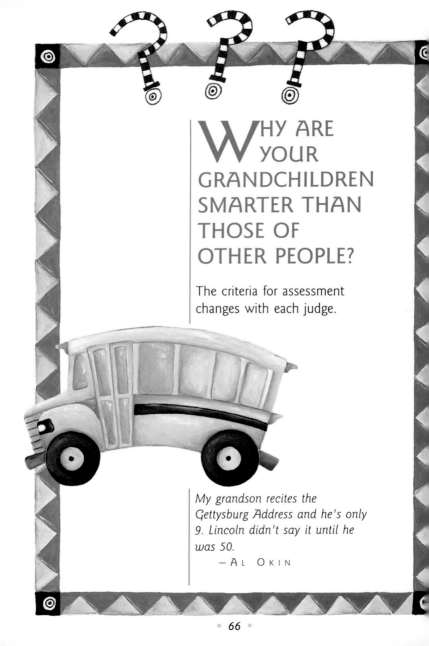

WHY ARE YOUR GRANDCHILDREN SMARTER THAN THOSE OF OTHER PEOPLE?

The criteria for assessment changes with each judge.

My grandson recites the Gettysburg Address and he's only 9. Lincoln didn't say it until he was 50.

— AL OKIN

WHAT'S THE DIFFERENCE BETWEEN HAPPINESS AND JOY?

Joy is the most infallible sign of the presence of God.
— LEON BLOY

Happiness happens from the outside; it depends on other people, events, results. Joy bubbles up from inside; it originates with attitude.

Happiness is in the circumstances; joy is in the heart. Happiness may not happen; joy is a promise from God.

IS THERE ANYTHING GOD CAN'T FORGIVE?

Nothing. Except unbelief.

Our God has a big eraser.
— BILLY ZEOLI

WHY IS THE GRASS ALWAYS GREENER ON THE OTHER SIDE OF THE FENCE?

The eight-year-old can't wait until he has the freedom of a teenager—his own wheels, his own friends, his own fun. The retired adult, shackled by a poor health, longs to have the energy and opportunities of an eight-year-old.

Each decade looks different on the front end. So we label the upcoming one "better"—until we get there. That same thinking holds true on the job. The clerk wants to be in management, with big perks and power. The executive drags home at night with a briefcase full of paperwork, toying with the idea of going back to a "simpler" job.

Likewise with relationships. When we're lonely, we long for intimate friends. When we're feeling put upon, we wish our relationships were less demanding. Married couples want the freedom and choices of being single; singles want the security and companionship of marriage.

Life is a direction, not a destination. All we need do to live in better times is to change our outlook on the present. Gratitude clears the road noise, cuts through the congestion, and gives us new perspective.

WILL WE KNOW EACH OTHER IN HEAVEN?

We'll have new bodies. Whether we'll recognize each other by personality, behavior, or spirit is not addressed in the Bible. But come to think of it, many of us who live together on earth don't really know each other.

The man who expects to go to heaven must take the time to study the route that will get him there.
— ANONYMOUS

The beauty that transcends time is the beauty of spirit. Beauty is charm, depth, wit, and warmth—all focused on the other person. Others feel it when they've been around it. These are the beautiful people of the world—and the happiest. True beauty is never open to interpretation by onlookers.

WHAT IS TRUE BEAUTY?

Nothing is more beautiful than cheerfulness in an old face.
— J. P. RICHTER

Beauty, unaccompanied by virtue, is as a flower without perfume.
— FRENCH PROVERB

WHY DO COUNTRIES WAGE WAR?

War is always brutal, often stupid, and sometimes just. On a positive note, we see the most noble virtues displayed by soldiers and their nations: faith, courage, endurance, sacrifice. On the negative side, we face loss so great that it cannot be counted or felt until generations later. In its noblest form, military power keeps madmen from creating mayhem for mankind.

It is only a generation after a war that the ordinary people begin to admit that it was a futile, foolish, and unnecessary one—which is something the prophets, poets, and philosophers were nearly stoned for saying as it began.
— SYDNEY HARRIS

WHAT IS THE DIFFERENCE BETWEEN A TRIAL AND A TEMPTATION?

A trial tests your faith and commitment. It's a burden that others pray you will endure, overcome, and learn from. Victory comes from passing through it successfully.

A temptation tugs at your roots. It's a trap that others pray you'll escape. Victory comes from avoiding it altogether or running from it swiftly.

WHY DOES PEER PRESSURE CLAIM SO MANY LIVES?

People need approval like plants need the sunlight. But yielding control of your life to the decisions of a peer panel can do to you what too much sun can do to a plant. Your life can become dry, shriveled, and eventually black.

The man who has no inner life is the slave of his surroundings.
— HENRI FREDERIC AMIEL

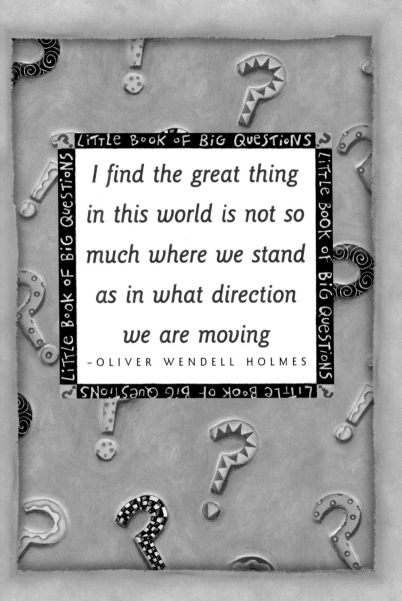

LITTLE BOOK OF BIG QUESTIONS

I find the great thing in this world is not so much where we stand as in what direction we are moving

-OLIVER WENDELL HOLMES

WHY BE GOOD?

Goodness is its own reward. It is interwoven with joy, peace, and gratitude in the fabric of life. Although it can be tinged with suffering, sacrifice, and sadness, goodness penetrates the coldest hearts and fuels the warmest moments for bystanders who see it in action.

You can always tell when you're on the road to righteousness—it's uphill.
— ERNEST
  BLEVINS

WHY DO SO MANY PEOPLE HAVE LOW SELF-ESTEEM?

They let the world—abusive, ignorant, or uncaring spouses, bosses, parents, or children— tell them what they're worth. A strong sense of self-esteem results from understanding the worth God places on a single life. That self-esteem blossoms and grows as we develop the attitudes, determination, knowledge, and skills that make others notice and appreciate our contributions in the world.

A strong self-esteem does not demand that society lower the standards. Rather, it demands that we raise our aim.

What is man that You are mindful of him, and the son of man that You visit him? For You have made him a little lower than the angels, and you have crowned him with glory and honor.
—PSALM 8:4-5

WHAT'S THE BEST WAY TO DEAL WITH DISAPPOINTMENT?

Disappointments come with daily living and divine appointments. Realize that disappointment may simply be a turn in the road before you see the real finish line. The truth is, most delights are sweeter after passing through disappointments along the way. It also helps to remember that getting what you expected may not be what you really wanted.

You cannot change the past, and you can't always control the present, but you can push the past into its proper perspective and you can face the present realistically.
— HUGH P. FELLOWS

WHAT DO WE LEARN FROM FAILURE?

Failure never becomes fatal until you fail on the inside. You learn to pick yourself up, dust things off, kick out of the way whatever you tripped over, refocus on the destination or change paths, and appreciate the destination once you reach it. Most important, you learn that you don't control the roads, the universe, or the travelers that pass you on the way.

Failure should be our teacher, not our undertaker. Failure is delay, not defeat. It is a temporary detour, not a dead-end street.
— WILLIAM A. WARD

WHAT'S THE NOBLEST PROFESSION OF ALL?

The noblest profession in life is one that allows you to use all your talents,

    most of the time,

        for many of the nicest people,

            to achieve meaningful results.

The worst profession in life is one in which you can work for a lifetime and earn nothing but money.

*Happiness is the result of being
too busy to be miserable.*
— ANONYMOUS

WHEN WILL THE WORLD END?

Nobody knows.

But of that day and hour no one knows, not even the angels of heaven, but My Father only.

—MATTHEW 24:36

WHY DO SO MANY PEOPLE WITH THE SAME VALUES AND BELIEF SYSTEM HOLD DIFFERENT OPINIONS ON SOCIAL ISSUES?

All Scripture is given by inspiration of God, and is profitable for doctrine, for reproof, for correction, for instruction in righteousness.
— 2 TIMOTHY 3 : 1 6

The Bible is infallible; human reasoning is not. The Bible provides principles that must be interpreted and applied to specific situations at hand. We approach interpretation with several obstacles: flawed translations, nuances of complex language, preconceived notions, limited insight, and errors in judgment.

The greatest difficulty of all? Listening to each other.

WHAT'S THE WORST PAIN IN THE WORLD?

Is it losing a child? Losing a parent? Losing your friend? Losing your reputation? Losing your health? Losing love? Losing all hope? Have you ever had a toothache spread from the tooth, to the jaw, to the entire head, until your whole consciousness could think of nothing but the pain? The same is true of emotional pain; after awhile, unchecked, the pain permeates your entire being.

How soon and how quickly you recover often depends on how many friends you have holding you up under the weight.

The most frustrating thing about unwelcome and chronic pain is its mandate to revise your life. Revision takes a measure of acceptance. And to accept it feels too much like abandoning independence.
— CAROLYN HARDESTY

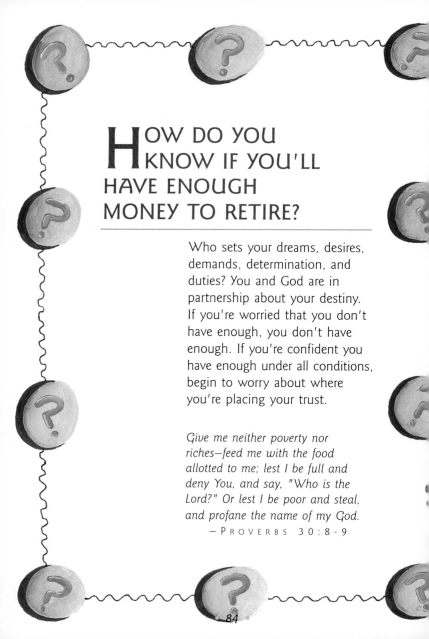

HOW DO YOU KNOW IF YOU'LL HAVE ENOUGH MONEY TO RETIRE?

Who sets your dreams, desires, demands, determination, and duties? You and God are in partnership about your destiny. If you're worried that you don't have enough, you don't have enough. If you're confident you have enough under all conditions, begin to worry about where you're placing your trust.

Give me neither poverty nor riches—feed me with the food allotted to me; lest I be full and deny You, and say, "Who is the Lord?" Or lest I be poor and steal, and profane the name of my God.
— PROVERBS 30:8-9

WHAT WAS GOOD ABOUT THE GOOD OLD DAYS?

A slower pace, a lower light bill, tastier food, a safer neighborhood, a less demanding family, leaders that lead—and a short memory.

> *The past always looks better than it was; it's only pleasant because it isn't here.*
>
> —FINLEY P. DUNNE

WHY IS IT SO HARD TO ACCEPT CHANGE?

Change brings challenges. Even when seated on a soft cushion, if you don't change your position occasionally, you become uncomfortable. Even changes from worse to better may bruise you. Think how hard it is for you to change yourself, and you'll understand the difficulty in changing an entire society.

Like clocks, successful businesses, people, and communities run down unless they're rewound.

Little men with little minds and little imagination jog through life in little ruts, smugly resisting all changes which would jar their little worlds.

— MARIE
FRASER

WHY DO RUMORS AND GOSSIP TRAVEL SO FAST?

With the speed of the Internet, propelled by the engines of stupidity, malice, or mirth, half-baked information and idle tales can destroy reputations, disrupt families, separate friends, and bankrupt businesses. Little minds gain satisfaction in passing on things quickly—before they learn the whole truth.

Wise men talk because they have something to say; fools, because they have to say something.
— PLATO

If there is a rumor in the air about you, you'd better treat it as you would a wasp: either ignore it or kill it with the first blow. Anything else will just stir it up.
— JAMES THOM

Gaining knowledge is admirable.

Quoting great principles is admirable.

Observing and learning from the lives of others is admirable.

Committing this knowledge, these principles, and this experience to your own life is wisdom.

WHAT IS TRUE WISDOM?

The fear of the LORD is the beginning of wisdom.
— PROVERBS 9:10

Heads that are filled with knowledge and wisdom have little space left for conceit.
— ANONYMOUS

WHAT IS THE BEST RESPONSE TO AN INSULT?

If you can, ignore it.

If you can't ignore it, sidestep it.

If you can't sidestep it, laugh at it.

If you can't laugh at it, listen to it.

If you can't listen to it, determine if it's true.

If it's true, change things.

> *Insults are the arguments
> employed by those who are
> in the wrong.*
> — ROUSSEAU

WHAT'S THE BEST RESPONSE TO GOSSIP?

Choose one:

- "I'm surprised to hear you say that; she speaks so highly of you."

- "That's not been my experience with him."

- "I rarely accept things that I don't know for a fact; somehow they usually get garbled going through so many people."

- "I guess it's best not to talk about it and make the situation even worse."

- "You never know—there could be a grain of truth in there somewhere."

- "I'm glad it's not your life or mine that's under such scrutiny at the moment."

- A disappointed or blank stare.

Gossip is when you must hurry and tell someone before you find out it isn't true.
— ANONYMOUS

WHO MAKES UP THE RULES ABOUT ETIQUETTE—WHAT'S POLITE, WHAT'S RUDE, WHAT'S ACCEPTABLE, AND WHAT'S NOT?

Rules are a misnomer. Etiquette is about observations. We observe how the civil and successful among us behave to get the results they want while helping others feel positive and have what they want. Following the "rules of etiquette" involves mimicking those same behaviors for the same results. Etiquette embodies what's acceptable to most of the people most of the time.

Good manners have much to do with emotions. To make them ring true, one must feel them, not merely exhibit them.
— AMY VANDERBILT

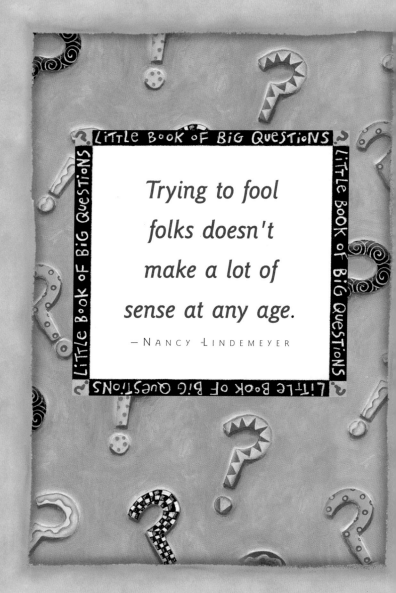

Trying to fool
folks doesn't
make a lot of
sense at any age.

— NANCY LINDEMEYER

WHAT'S THE BEST WAY TO TEACH CHILDREN?

By example—live the principles and progress you want to see portrayed in their lives.

Every word and deed of a parent is a fiber woven into the character of a child, which ultimately determines how that child fits into the fabric of society.
— DAVID WILKERSON

WHAT DO GRANDCHILDREN CONTRIBUTE TO YOUR LIFE?

Grandchildren turn your head, swell your pride, lift your chin, drain your energy, and make you eat your words. Most important, however, they give you a second chance to correct mistakes, spend quality time, and love them without the responsibility of teaching a lesson when they'd rather not learn it.

Your sons weren't made to like you. That's what grandchildren are for.
— JANE SMILEY

Have you noticed that few grandchildren carry photos of their grandparents with them? Instead, they carry their undivided attention, their unconditional love, their best wisdom, and their fondest hopes stamped on their heart.

WHAT DO GRANDPARENTS CONTRIBUTE TO THE LIVES OF THEIR GRANDCHILDREN?

Our children are not going to be just "our children"—they are going to be other people's husbands and wives and the parents of our grandchildren.

— DR. MARY CALDERONE

How Fast Can You Grow a Grateful Heart?

Have you ever hit a single keystroke on your computer and wiped out an entire file that you didn't intend to destroy? Can you feel that sinking sensation in the pit of your stomach? The pressure of distress against your rib cage? The swell of nausea as you realize that you've deleted a month's work?

Once we realize that with that same swiftness of a keystroke, we can lose everything—health, family, money—gratitude grows deeper.

An interesting phenomenon in children is that gratitude or thankfulness comes relatively late in their young lives. They almost have to be taught it; if not, they are apt to grow up thinking that the world owes them a living.

— FULTON J. SHEEN

How do you know when you're getting old?

- You don't mind telling your age—but you don't remember it.

- You'd rather hear about things than do them.

- People give you a hand rather than hand you a gift.

- People start to listen to your advice.

- Where ideas are concerned, you see more shades of gray.

- You meet fewer morons, bigots, or rascals; you even suspect some of them might be as right as you are.

- You have more friends in heaven than on earth.

Age seldom arrives smoothly or quickly. It's more often a succession of jerks.
— JEAN RHYS

WHAT'S SO BAD ABOUT GETTING INTO DEBT?

You lose things: sleep, family, control—and self-esteem when you can't get out. Once upon a time we had to work hard to save money. Now it's difficult just to stay even—to stay broke without going into debt.

As a general rule, prosperity is what keeps us in debt.
—ANONYMOUS

WHY DO PEOPLE WHO BORROW MONEY FROM YOU BECOME FORMER FRIENDS FAST?

Debt makes people uncomfortable around their benefactors. They either feel embarrassed because they had to borrow, disadvantaged because you have the money to lend, discouraged because they can't repay it fast enough, or guilty because they are unwilling to repay it at all. Pretty soon, they're looking for a slight or insult from you that will explain their condition or justify their attitude.

If you have to borrow, always borrow from a pessimist. He doesn't expect to be paid anyway.
— ANONYMOUS

Consider the theory of relativity. Time flies when you're making memories; it drags when you're ironing denim. It flies when you're eating lemon meringue; it drags when you're scratching the label off a jar. It flies when you're on vacation; it drags when you're in the hospital.

Which is reality—the minutes or only our thinking during the minutes? How old would you be if you aged by pleasant memories rather than calendar years?

WHY DOES A WEEK ON A DIET FEEL LONGER THAN A WEEK ON VACATION?

For a moment, consider that maybe that very thing is happening. Some people come to the end of their life feeling full and satisfied. Others come to the end of their life feeling as though they've never lived. They stare at an imminent death as if they've been shortchanged.

If we want to lengthen our lives, we should make an effort to build more pleasant memories. At the very least, the result would be less mental wear and tear.

WHY DOES THE MEDIA REPORT MORE BAD NEWS THAN GOOD NEWS?

The media says bad news sells. Readers and listeners say bad news bombards and distresses them. Obviously, somebody's not listening.

What a scarcity of news there would be if everyone obeyed the Ten Commandments!

— ANONYMOUS

How is Christianity Different From Other Religions?

Christianity is the only religion based on evidence of a personal God who rose from the dead.

The problem with Christianity is not that it has been tried and found wanting, but that it has been found difficult, and left untried.
— G. K. CHESTERTON

WHY DO YOUNG CHILDREN SUFFER AND DIE?

Those who have suffered understand suffering and therefore extend their hand.
— PATTI SMITH

Children are often the great teachers in any society. Through their pain, they teach us patience. Through their helplessness, they teach us dependence and unselfishness. Through their acceptance, they teach us trust. Through their dying, they teach us grace and love.

At best, adults label death "natural" and at it's worse, bad. Children hold no such prejudices. Heaven is the early reward for our greatest teachers.

Compassion is
a foundation for
sharing our aliveness
and building a
more human world.

—MARTIN LOWENTHAL

WHY DO SOME CULTURES VALUE AGING AND OTHER CULTURES DESPISE IT?

Some cultures value knowledge, experience, wisdom, confidence, steadfastness, patience, and perspective. Other cultures value innocence, pleasing appearance, risk-taking, energy, spontaneity, and optimism. Age is often attached to each set of traits.

Many people think old age is a disease, something to be thwarted if possible. But someone has said that if any period is a disease, it is youth. Age is recovering from it.

— T. C. MYERS

HOW DO YOU KNOW IF GOD IS TRYING TO TEACH YOU PATIENCE?

- Traffic slows down when you switch lanes.

- It always rains after you wash your car.

- You always come up one sock short after washing.

- When you drop toast, it always lands buttered-side down.

Your car stops knocking only when you drive it into the repair shop.

If these sound familiar to your experience, remember this: patience strengthens your resolve, tames the temper, sweetens the disposition, replaces pride, and locks the jaw.

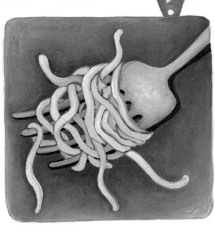

WHY ARE ALL THE GOOD-TASTING FOODS BAD FOR YOU?

Refined. Irradiated. Canned. Bottled. Vacuum-packed. Frozen. Dried. Dehydrated. Bleached. Smoked. Sprayed. Injected. Dyed. Waxed. Conditioned. Emulsified. Synthesized. Stabilized. Pasteurized. Tenderized. Hydrolized. Homogenized. Pretend you're a carrot for a moment—how much energy would you have left to burn or taste? No wonder half the population in America stays on a diet. You might as well eat bland as bad.

I want nothing to do with natural foods. At my age I need all the preservatives I can get.

— GEORGE BURNS

HOW DO YOU BECOME FINANCIALLY INDEPENDENT?

- Educate yourself about money and its management. Know what you have, what you need, and what you want.

- Save ten percent of everything you earn.

- Live beneath your means. Simplify, get the best value you can, and enjoy what you have.

- Get what you pay for. Pay attention to detail. Demand quality. Be fair, but firm.

- Build an emergency fund for the unexpected: vacations, wheel realignments, gall bladder surgery, a friend's wedding.

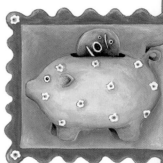

- Do not borrow money on anything that decreases in value while you own it.

- Invest your money regularly, carefully, and patiently.

- Plan for the future: retirement, wills, gifts, taxes.

- Give at least ten percent to God's work.

American men are obsessed with money. American women are obsessed with weight. The men talk of gain, the women talk of loss, and I do not know which talk is the more boring."

— M A R Y A
M A N N E S

HOW MUCH MONEY IS ENOUGH?

The American lifestyle takes money, no doubt about it. Debts are about the only thing we can get without cold hard cash. Nothing tests your character, your courage, and your commitment like suddenly making or losing a large sum of money. Fools sometimes make money, but sometimes money makes fools.

Is your quest for money making you healthier, happier, and wiser? If not, stop building your bank account and start building a life.

You aren't wealthy until you have something money can't buy.
— GARTH BROOKS

The more you have to live for, the less you need to live on. Those who make acquisition their goal never have enough.
— SYDNEY HARRIS

WHY DO YOU FEEL NOSTALGIC ON YOUR BIRTHDAY?

We often get nostalgic about things that weren't so good in the present tense. But birthdays cause us to take stock of our years and see how closely our days have followed our dreams.

It [aging] doesn't happen all at once.
You become. It takes a long time
— MARGERY WILLIAMS

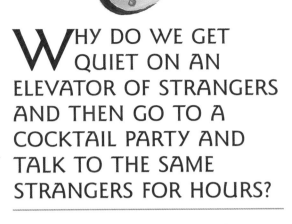

WHY DO WE GET QUIET ON AN ELEVATOR OF STRANGERS AND THEN GO TO A COCKTAIL PARTY AND TALK TO THE SAME STRANGERS FOR HOURS?

We need permission to get into other people's emotional space. At a party, you have permission to engage others; in elevators, you don't. Not to mention, most people feel timid about talking to strangers. They need a party to force them to become momentarily uncomfortable for the sake of becoming more comfortable long-term.

In our 20's we wear a mask; we pretend to know more than we do. We must be willing, as we get older, to shed cocktail party phoniness and admit, "I am who I am."

— GAIL SHEEHY

WHEN SHOULD YOU RETIRE?

Beware of this common experience in retirement: waking up in the morning feeling as though you have nothing to do and going to bed at night feeling as though you got only half of it done. Consider retirement when you have three foundations in place:

- something to live on,
- someone or something to live for,
- and someone to think you're somebody.

It's only possible to live happily ever after on a day-to-day basis.

— MARGARET BONNANO